DANIEL BOONE

by LILIAN MOORE

Illustrated by WILLIAM MOYERS

Prepared under the supervision of JOSETTE FRANK,
Children's Book Adviser of the Child Study Association of America

Manufactured in the United States of America
1 2 3 4 5 6 7 8 9 0

RANDOM HOUSE · NEW YORK

THE BOY HUNTER

More than anything else in the world, young Daniel wanted a rifle.

"When you are twelve, Dan," his father had promised, "you shall have your rifle."

But this summer Daniel was only ten. Maybe not old enough to have his own rifle, but old enough to know that he'd rather be roaming in the woods with a gun than be almost anywhere else he could think of; old enough to know that for him there was a special happiness to be found in the deep forests that surrounded his home.

Home was the Boone farm in Pennsylvania where Daniel had been born in November, 1734. (Just about two and a half years earlier a boy named George Washington had been born farther south in Virginia.) The Boone farm wasn't anything like the rich rolling farmlands you'll find in Pennsylvania today. It was really a clearing in the woods, part of a small frontier settlement called Oley Township, and it had been chopped out of the Pennsylvania forest by the sharp axes and strong backs of the Boone family.

Daniel helped on the farm, of course. Everybody helped when there was so much to do to keep alive and so few hands to do it.

But it wasn't farming Daniel cared about.

His father, Squire Boone, was not only a farmer but a blacksmith, too. In the flames of his forge he shaped and welded the pieces of metal he needed to mend his neighbors' wagons, or repair their broken rifles and bear traps. Watching his father at work, Daniel learned ways of handling metal that he remembered all his life.

But it wasn't mending wagons in a smithy's shop that young Daniel cared about.

Squire Boone was not only a farmer and a blacksmith but a weaver, too. That's what Dan's grandfather, George Boone, had been—a weaver. In the Boones' log cabin there were six looms in which "homespun" was made, cloth the Boones sold to their neighbors or sent to market in the nearby city of Philadelphia. Watching those endlessly busy looms, Dan learned all about making cloth.

But it wasn't weaving that Daniel cared about.

He was only ten, but Daniel Boone already knew that what he wanted to do most of all was to wander, hunt, and explore in the green and quiet woodlands all around him.

Daniel was lucky, too, that there was so much time for wandering in the forests that summer. His father had just bought twenty-five more acres of grazing land for his cows. This land was too far from the Boone farm for the cows to be taken back and forth every day. So ten-year-old Daniel was the one chosen among his many brothers and sisters to go with his mother to live for the summer in a cabin on the new land and help her care for the cows.

When the cows were milked and the butter churned or the cheese made, and the morning's chores all done, the cows were turned loose. So, in a way, was young Dan. He was supposed to keep his eye on the cows and round them up at the end of the day. But meanwhile he was free, free to go wandering through the woods.

As he roamed through the forest that summer, Daniel saw game of every kind—deer, wild turkey, squirrel, chipmunk, bear. To the pioneer family, game was food. It was welcome meat at the table in a world where there was no butcher shop just around the corner.

Daniel longed for the rifle that would be his when he was twelve. Twelve! His father might as well have said twenty for all the good that was this summer. Daniel wanted to hunt right away.

He found a way. Too young for a rifle, he made his own weapon. He looked around until he found a sapling that was just right. Then he pulled up the little tree, and whittled away with his knife. And when he was done cutting the branches and shaping the hard knobbed roots, he had a fine spear!

Daniel practised throwing his spear until he was sure he wouldn't miss. Then he went hunting. It was a proud moment when he appeared for the first time at the door of the little cabin, and held up the wild turkey and rabbit he had brought home for his mother's cooking pot— brought down in the forest with his home-made spear!

When Daniel was twelve, he got his rifle. That was a day to make a boy feel like a man! Now there was no holding back the young hunter.

Every summer, until he was sixteen, he went back to live in the log cabin to help his mother with the cows. No need any more to make spears out of saplings! Now Dan roamed through the woods with his gun at his side, his eye growing keener and his hand steadier on the rifle every day. These were happy summers, but it was the winter hunting season Daniel really looked forward to. Then he went off with his rifle, exploring the forests and mountains near his home until he knew them as well as a boy today knows the streets of his home town. Soon it was Dan the family depended on for their supply of meat. The skins and furs were sold for much needed money or supplies.

In the woods where Daniel's family lived there was no school. Daniel was taught reading, writing, and arithmetic at home. His mother and his big brother Sam's wife Sarah took turns teaching him. It must have been hard for Dan, longing for the freedom of the woods, to sit still and learn his lessons.

Spelling was the hardest of all. Daniel just couldn't seem to put his mind on it. Even Uncle John Boone took a hand in the spelling lessons. It was Uncle John who complained to Dan's father about the poor spelling. But Squire Boone must have understood his son. "Let the girls do the spelling," he told Uncle John, "and Dan will do the shooting."

Dan couldn't get interested in spelling, but in the school he really loved there was no better pupil. He learned every lesson the forest could teach—everything a man would ever need to know to keep alive in the trackless wilderness. He learned to stand so still that not a leaf revealed his presence. He learned to move through the forest without leaving a single footprint or sign that he had gone by. He learned to swing to safety on hanging vines, and to find his way home through the gloomy forest guided by a spot of sunlight on some leaves or the thickness of the bark on one side of a tree.

He learned to tell the tracks of a bear or deer or wildcat, and to answer the cry of a panther or the hoot of an owl. Where others saw only shadows in the forest, he saw its busy life, and where for others there was only the frightening silence of the deep woods, it spoke to him with a hundred different voices.

By the time he was sixteen, there was no better woodsman in all of eastern Pennsylvania than young Daniel Boone.

THE BOONES MOVE ON

It took all kinds of people to build America. Among the early settlers some families were "stayers" and some were "movers." The stayers came to the settlements and put down their roots. There they lived, raised their families, built up their land, and died. But the movers were always pushing ahead, always moving from the land that was settled to the land that wasn't.

The Boones were movers—from Grandfather Boone, who had left a comfortable home in England, right down to Daniel's own grandsons. It is easy enough to believe the story that the great scout Kit Carson was one of Dan Boone's grandsons.

Before Daniel was seventeen, the Boones were on their way out of Pennsylvania to a new home somewhere "southwest." Squire Boone had heard about the rich land down in North Carolina, so the Boones packed up and set off, the women and children riding in the wagons with the family's belongings, the menfolk on horseback and on foot, driving the unhappy cows before them. The cows were "stayers." They'd have been perfectly satisfied to munch Pennsylvania grass for the rest of their lives.

It was a long, slow, and hard journey. Even the Boones weren't sure where it would end. Daniel acted as scout and hunter as they headed across Pennsylvania, down the Cumberland Valley to Virginia, and then at last into North Carolina.

There in the rich valley of the Yadkin River, Squire Boone found what he wanted. They had gone five hundred miles from the farm in

Pennsylvania, and the journey had taken almost two years. Once again the Boones began the back-breaking work of building a home in the woods—clearing the land of trees and stumps and stones, building a log cabin, ploughing the land, putting in a crop of corn and potatoes.

They were really on the frontier now, right at the end of the white man's world. Even the "movers" had had to stop here. For to the west rose a great wall of mountains whose secrets were known only to the Indians. The mountains seemed to say: "Go no farther, white men! This is the Indians' hunting ground." Looking up at those mountains day after day, Daniel wondered: What lay beyond them? What was it like out there in the Wilderness? It was a wondering that did not stop.

Meanwhile, Daniel was happy in his new home. It was full of every kind of game—bear, muskrat, deer, beaver, elk—and soon he was known throughout the Yadkin Valley for his skill in hunting. Those first years in North Carolina were busy, pleasant ones for Young Dan.

But there was trouble ahead.

War.

War with the French and the Indians.

DANIEL LEARNS A LESSON

Indians had always been part of Daniel's world. Even as a young child he had seen Indians of the Delaware tribes come down from their villages into the settlement where the Boones lived. Right "next door" on Grandfather Boone's farm he had seen them come as welcome visitors.

And of course Dan had often met Indians in his boyhood wanderings through the woods. He had watched carefully the way they moved through the forest, never stirring a leaf or breaking a twig, their tawny

bodies gliding through patches of sunlight and forest shadows with marvelous swiftness. Watching, he had learned some of the ways in which a man might become part of the forest itself.

He even learned to think like an Indian. In later years, there were many times when Daniel Boone was able to save his own life and the lives of others because he seemed to know just what the Indians would do next. "This is the trail they will take," he would say, or "This is the plan they will follow." And most of the time he was right.

While Daniel was growing up, he heard tales of sudden and terrible Indian raids on other frontier settlements. But the Indians that Daniel knew as a boy were always friendly. The Boones were Quakers, and they lived in a Quaker settlement. The Quakers were a peaceful people. They were fair and friendly in their dealings with the Indians. The Indians, in turn, had feelings of friendship for the Quakers. They even came down from the hills one day dressed in war paint (probably scaring everyone in the settlement out of his wits!) because they had heard that some other Indians were about to attack their white friends and they wanted to protect them. Luckily, it was a false alarm.

Daniel met his first unfriendly Indian in the Yadkin Valley. At the same time he learned an important lesson. The men of the frontier were very proud of their shooting, and they enjoyed having contests to find

out which among them were the best shots. Sometimes they would
gather to see who could drive a nail with one bullet, or snuff out the
flame of a candle, or hit a tiny mark on a tree trunk without missing
once.

In several of these games Daniel had shot better than an Indian brave
of the Catawba tribe who was known as Saucy Jack. The Indian was
terribly angry. A friend came hurrying to tell Dan's father, "Saucy Jack

is going around saying he'll kill Daniel!" Squire Boone knew that Daniel was away on a hunting trip. Suppose Saucy Jack trailed him there and tried to kill the unsuspecting Daniel! Squire Boone reached for his hatchet. "I'll be first!" he cried, and went out looking for Saucy Jack.

Perhaps Saucy Jack thought it wiser to stay out of the old man's way, for Squire Boone never did find him.

But Daniel learned something from this experience that he did not forget. The Indians were sensitive, and proud of their skills, and to be

beaten in contests by a white man was an insult. After that, Daniel remembered never again to lose the friendship of an Indian by shooting better than he did.

Before long Daniel had more to worry about than one unfriendly Indian. The clouds of war had been gathering darkly along the frontier. Now they burst, and Dan Boone had his first taste of real warfare.

The most important action that the British planned was the capture of Fort Duquesne. The French had built this fort where Pittsburgh stands today. And Daniel Boone, at that time almost twenty-one, keen-eyed, sun-browned, lean and strong, answered the call for volunteers from North Carolina to join in the march against the French and their Indian allies.

It was a strange army that Daniel joined. There were woodsmen like himself in moccasins, fringed buckskin jackets and leggings, and there were British "regulars" splendid in their fine and fancy redcoats. The red-coated soldiers marched and drilled and drilled and marched, until Daniel, watching them, must have wondered, "Whatever kind of Indian fighting is this going to be?"

There was another soldier in that army, a young officer, who must have wondered, too. For Colonel George Washington had already had some experience in fighting the French and Indians.

In charge of this army was General Braddock, fresh from the shores of England where there were no Indians. He was full of scorn for the backwoodsmen who wore buckskins instead of red coats and who knew little and cared less about the fine soldierly business of drilling. General Braddock himself was a brave man and a good fighter, but the men who knew how to fight the Indians couldn't tell him because he wouldn't listen.

If Daniel thought that he was going to be a fleet-footed scout, leading the way for the others, he was certainly disappointed. As the army journeyed slowly up a mountain path so narrow it had to be hacked out yard by yard, Daniel found himself well in the rear, bumping along as a wagon driver.

But then something happened that turned out to be one of the most important events of his life.

He met John Finley.

DANIEL HEARS ABOUT KENTUCKY

John Finley was a trader and a hunter, and he had been on the other side of those mountains that rose to the west of Yadkin like a wall.

John Finley had been in the Wilderness!

Wide-eyed, Daniel listened to the stories he had to tell. As he jogged along in the rear of the army, or sat around the campfires at night, John Finley talked and Daniel Boone listened.

Yes, John told him, he'd gone real deep into the mountains, trading with the Indians. He'd even been as far as the Indian villages on the Ohio River.

What was it like, Dan wanted to know. What was it like out there?

Truly a paradise! the trader told him. The most beautiful country he'd ever seen. Great forests. Soil so rich that everything grew green and tall.

And the hunting? Dan leaned forward with excitement as he asked about the hunting.

John Finley could hardly find words to tell of the game that roamed in those mountains. Deer everywhere, beaver, otter, thousands of buffalo! More wild geese and ducks than a man could count! It was a land to dream about, John Finley said. The Indians called it Kentucky.

Daniel was filled with an eagerness to see this land for himself. Could they, perhaps, go hunting there together?

John Finley thought it was a fine idea. That's what they would do, hunt there together some day real soon.

Meanwhile, Braddock's army was approaching Fort Duquesne. The soldiers leading the march were only ten miles from their goal. Then suddenly the French and their Indian allies struck. Hidden in the dense woods, they let loose a rain of bullets. The fancy red coats of the British soldiers made wonderful targets, and the drilling and marching were of no use at all. It was a bloody battle and a terrible defeat for the British. General Braddock was killed, and those who could do so fled in retreat.

For Dan, as he cut his horse loose from the wagon and galloped away, it must have been a day full of horror.

But he had learned a lot.

He had learned something about fighting Indians.

Best of all, he had learned about Kentucky.

JOHN FINLEY AGAIN!

Almost fourteen years went by, and Daniel's dream of going up into the mountains to Kentucky was still only a dream.

Many things had happened in those years.

Back home in the Yadkin Valley, after Braddock's defeat, Daniel had married Rebecca Bryan, the tall dark-eyed girl who lived near the Boone farm. And now their sons and daughters were growing up. James was the oldest; he'd been hunting with his father since he was eight years old.

In winter, when the woods grew cold, Dan used to tuck his son right inside his own hunting shirt and keep him snug and warm. James was already a fine woodsman. It made Dan proud to see how he could creep up on a deer without a sound, then "freeze" to the stillness of a tree rooted in the earth, his hand steady on the rifle as he aimed.

There had been plenty of Indian fighting in those years, too, for the powerful Cherokee tribes, once so friendly to the English settlers, had become savage enemies, determined to wipe them out. Daniel Boone was a good Indian fighter but he never fought Indians just for the sake of killing them. In the times in which he lived, he had to fight Indians to stay alive himself. But there were many Indians he respected who respected him, too.

There were men on the frontier, however, who feared and hated all Indians. They welcomed the chance to "kill an Indian." And it was just such a cruel and needless killing of some friendly Cherokee braves that had turned these tribes from friend to foe and sent them from their peace pipes to their tomahawks.

When the Cherokees had been defeated and the fighting ended, Daniel went back to his hunting. But just as Boone, the Indian fighter, never killed Indians just for the sake of killing, so Daniel Boone, greatest of American hunters, never killed game that he did not need to kill. Years later when he had a chance to help make some laws, the first law he asked for was one to protect wild life from hunters who killed without caring. Dan loved the forest and respected the life it sheltered.

To provide for his large family Daniel hunted deer and trapped beaver. The deer meat—venison—was food; the skins and furs were sold. Buckskin clothing was the "uniform" of the frontiersmen, and the skin of the male deer, the buck, was usually worth more than that of the doe. It is odd to think that one of the few things Daniel Boone might recognize in our world today is our slang expression for money. Many a time he traded three doeskins for "two bucks." And of a beaver skin he himself may have said, "This one is worth three bucks!"

As Daniel hunted season after season, he went deeper and deeper into the mountains around North Carolina—not to the north where Kentucky lay, but over mountain ranges to the part of the wilderness that was Tennessee. He hunted with friends, and he hunted with his sons, but most of the time he seemed content to hunt alone.

Sometimes, on the bark of beech trees, he left word that he had passed by. In the woods that had been his school as a boy, these beech trees were his writing slates. Once he carved a message: "Come on boys here's good water," and in eastern Tennessee there was a beech tree that stood for almost a hundred years with the words: "D. Boon cilled a bar on this tree, year 1760." (Dan was certainly better at hunting than at spelling!)

Many things had happened in those fourteen years; and Daniel Boone had roamed far and wide. But not to Kentucky. Not yet.

That was to come soon.

For one autumn day, quite by chance, a peddler with odds and ends to sell knocked at the door of the Boone cabin.

And the peddler was John Finley!

THE DREAM COMES TRUE

What a strange and lucky meeting that was!

How much John Finley and Daniel Boone must have had to tell each other after fourteen years!

John Finley stayed on with the Boones all winter, and in the long evenings he and Dan sat and talked in the Boone cabin as they once talked around a campfire—about Kentucky.

John told Daniel that he'd gone back to Kentucky by way of canoe down the Ohio River and back—a hard trip! But he had learned from the Indians that there was a secret opening somewhere through the wall of mountains. He'd heard, too, about a trail used by the Indians called the Warrior's Path. It would lead them into Kentucky if once they could find it! Did Daniel Boone and John Finley perhaps look at each other then with the same thought: *a good woodsman could find it?* Before that winter was over they had decided that in the spring they would make up an exploring party and set off for Kentucky.

There were six men in the party. On the first of May in 1769, they turned and waved goodbye to their friends and families, and set off on a journey that for Daniel was the beginning of a dream come true.

Daniel's brother-in-law John Stuart, whom Daniel loved as a brother, was one of the group. The other three men were friends from the Yadkin Valley.

Daniel's younger brother Squire—the one who had been named for their father—wanted to go, too. But someone had to stay home and harvest the crops, so it was planned that Squire would join the group later and bring fresh supplies. It was a strange and wonderful "date" that the Boone brothers made—to meet hundreds of miles away in a wilderness that neither one had ever seen!

Those who watched them go that day saw six men on horseback dressed in rough deerskin clothes. Each man was leading another horse with a pack saddle that carried supplies—salt, traps, kettles, blankets and bearskins, and enough food to last until the men could begin to hunt. They must have looked ready for every kind of danger. In their belts they wore tomahawks, hunting knives, and the powder horns and bullet pouches from which they loaded their guns. Across their shoulders they carried their long trusty rifles. Daniel's must have been that favorite gun he called "Tick-Licker!"

And so they were off—to the Wilderness. The Indians had given it the name Kentucky—"a pleasant meadow, a smiling land whence the river flows." But they also called it "a dark and bloody ground." Daniel Boone would learn that it was both.

For several weeks the travelers moved slowly through rough, wild country, crossing first one mountain range, then another. They were all good woodsmen, and soon they picked up a hunter's "trace"—a lightly marked trail. To Daniel Boone, who could find a tree he had marked in the forest twenty years after he had carved it, a trail must have been like a highway. This one led Daniel to the "secret" opening in the mountain wall. We know now that it was the Cumberland Gap, a natural gateway through the mountains where the three states of Virginia, Tennessee, and Kentucky meet.

Then the Warrior's Path was found, and Finley turned out to be right. For one fine spring day, Daniel Boone stood on a mountaintop and looked down. And there at last, stretching before him as far as he could see, more beautiful than he had dreamed, were the green and fertile lands, the noble forests, and the shining rivers of Kentucky!

Pushing ahead, the explorers made camp, and began to hunt. Right through the summer and autumn months, everything seemed fine. Kentucky was a hunter's heaven, and these were among the happiest days of Daniel's life. Month after month the hunters watched with satisfaction the growing piles of skins and furs that meant money for all of them.

Then the trouble began.

Daniel and John Stuart, out hunting together, were captured by the Indians—not once but twice! The first time they were forced to lead the band of Shawnees right to their camp and watch them take their precious skins and horses. Then the Shawnee chief said in English: "Now, brothers, go home and stay there. Don't come here any more, for this is the Indians' hunting ground, and all the animals, skins, and furs are ours. If you are so foolish as to come here again, you may be sure the wasps and yellow jackets will sting you severely!" He shook their hands and let them go.

Of course Daniel and Stuart did not go home. Instead they followed the Indians, and tried to get back their horses. Again they were caught. This time the Indians planned to take them along as prisoners. Daniel was very friendly and acted as if he were glad to be among his Indian brothers. As soon as they stopped guarding him so carefully, he and Stuart made their escape.

All this was too much for Finley and the others. Gone were their skins and furs, the work of months! They had been given warnings about the "sting of wasps!" And to top it all, they had almost lost Daniel and Stuart! They had had enough of Kentucky, and they headed back for the settlements at once.

Daniel and John Stuart were not alone very long. Just as the others left, Squire Boone arrived. He had come five hundred miles through the Wilderness to keep his date with Daniel! He brought fresh supplies and a friend named Neely.

The four men set up camp again and started hunting. But soon there was another terrible blow. John Stuart went out hunting as usual one day—but he never returned. The others searched until at last they had to give up. Stuart was never seen again.

This was too much for Neely. Now he, too, had had enough of the Wilderness. He, too, went back home to Carolina.

But Daniel and Squire Boone stayed on. They built a cabin and went on hunting and trapping until they had a good supply of furs— but very little ammunition left.

So back through the mountain forests went Squire Boone, back 500 miles to the settlements to sell the skins and get more ammunition and supplies. He made this trip twice, and each time—once for three months, the other time for two months—Daniel Boone was alone in the Wilderness.

What was it like to be alone in the Wilderness? To be, in Daniel's words, "with no bread, no salt, without a horse or a dog?"

There was danger.

There were Indian hunting parties all around, and the Indians had told Daniel plainly how they felt about the white men in Kentucky. Whenever Daniel thought they had discovered his camp, he would hide in the canebrake. These were great thickets of cane that grew like giant cornstalks, sometimes as high as two-story houses.

Daniel had some narrow escapes. Once, as he was exploring along a river, he looked up to find himself suddenly surrounded on three sides by Indians. On the fourth side was a steep cliff! Before the astonished Indians realized what had happened, Daniel had leaped off the cliff into the top of a sugar maple tree, let himself down through the branches, and disappeared!

At another time, in killing a buffalo for food, he frightened a whole herd, and they stampeded—right toward him! To escape, he hid behind a tree, while dozens of huge angry beasts roared past him on both sides of the tree.

There was adventure, too, the adventure of discovery.

In these lonely months, with little ammunition for hunting, Daniel began to explore Kentucky. Living in limestone caves and keeping out of the way of Indians, he ranged everywhere—north to the Ohio River, and as far west as the place where the city of Louisville stands today.

And there was happiness.

Sometimes, in spite of the danger, Daniel just had to burst into song in this beautiful world of green forests, fertile lands, and broad flowing streams. Here was a land where everything and everyone could "grow to a full size." It was a world he loved and understood.

One night he saw a campfire and, creeping up quietly, discovered Squire—returned from his second trip home!

The brothers continued to hunt for a while longer, and then in March, 1771 they turned toward home with a fine haul of skins. They were growing more cheerful every hour, for they had come a long way and soon they would be home. Then suddenly, not far from the settlement, they were attacked by Indians and robbed of all their skins and equipment.

After two years in the wilderness, Daniel Boone was returning home, empty handed and poorer than when he had left.

But no one could rob him of what he had seen. He knew Kentucky now, knew it as no other white man in America did.

And the "mover" was about ready to move again.

INDIANS STRIKE AGAIN

Kentucky was where Daniel Boone wanted to live. In Kentucky there was good, rich land so a man needn't feel poor—land enough so a man could feel free.

Two years after he returned from the Wilderness, Daniel made his first attempt to go back as a settler.

When he sold his farm in 1773 and started out with his family for Kentucky, five other families joined him. There were always people who were willing to follow Daniel Boone. Men, women, children (there were eight Boone children now!), pack horses loaded with household goods, pigs, stubborn cows that had to be coaxed to go—they all began to move slowly along the narrow mountain trails that Daniel knew so well.

They were still not too far from the Yadkin Valley when Daniel found out that they would need more flour and farm tools. Young James Boone was sent back to get these supplies. This first-born of Daniel's sons, this boy he was so proud of, was a fine young man of sixteen, and it seemed a simple enough journey for the young woodsman to make.

It would have been, too, except that on the way back, with darkness coming on, James and the others in the returning party camped for the night. Before morning they were attacked by a band of Indians. James and three others were savagely murdered.

Axes rang steadily as the men blazed trees and cut away underbrush, leveling the road as much as they could in rugged mountain country. When they reached southeastern Kentucky, they had to wrest every foot of the road from the Wilderness, chopping and burning their way through miles of dense woods and canebrake. Slowly they inched forward until they reached their destination—the spot that Daniel had long ago chosen as the place in the Wilderness where some day he would settle.

There on the banks of the Kentucky River they cleared the land and built the group of cabins that was to be known as Boonesborough. It was not the first settlement in Kentucky as Daniel may have dreamed it would be, but it was to be one of those brave outposts that never lowered its flag.

Then Daniel went back over the Wilderness Road, and when he returned again it was with his family. Proudly he spoke of "my wife and daughter being the first white women that ever stood on the banks of the Kentucky River . . ."

Women and children had come to live at Boonesborough. Now it was no longer just a fort and some cabins in the Wilderness. Now it was really a settlement!

THE YEARS OF DANGER

Exciting things were happening in the thirteen American colonies.

Men like Daniel Boone had pushed the American frontier westward; more and more settlers were heading for "Kaintuck." But within this frontier—back in the towns and villages of America, in cities like Boston and Philadelphia—people were pushing forward, too, in a different kind of struggle, in the fight to be free and independent of England.

Even as Daniel Boone and his men were building Boonesborough, Paul Revere was riding through the countryside of Massachusetts warning the people that British troops were coming. And before Boonesborough was finished, the Battle of Bunker Hill had been fought between American militia men and British soldiers in one of the early battles of the American Revolutionary War.

Now the British did what the French had done years before. In their war against the American colonists, they tried to win the Indians to their side, and stirred them up to attack the frontier settlements.

The Indians did not need much urging to attack the new settlements. They had their own continuing war with the American frontiersman. Now they saw with dread that the white men had come to the Wilderness itself—not just to hunt but to settle. Nothing seemed to stop them. They must be destroyed before it was too late, before the Indians were driven from Kentucky as they had already been driven from their other lands.

So for all the years of the Revolutionary War, while the other colonists were fighting the British, the settlers in the Kentucky Wilderness were fighting Indians.

Many who had come to the Kentucky that was "the smiling land" fled from the Kentucky that had indeed become a "dark and bloody ground."

But others, like the Boones, stood fast with their rifles against years of terrible Indian warfare. Perhaps they did not know, as they defended their lonely homes in the Wilderness, that they were also helping to hold the southern colonies against the British. They were helping America to win her War of Independence.

The Kentucky settlers lived with danger every minute of their lives. But sometimes they would forget.

One quiet summer Sunday afternoon at Boonesborough, Jemima Boone, Daniel's fourteen-year-old daughter, went out canoeing with her two friends, Betsy and Fanny Calloway. It was a lovely July day, and there hadn't been a sign of an Indian since the winter. The girls paddled a little, and then their canoe drifted slowly and gently across the river. As it reached the other shore, they found to their horror that five Indian braves had been hiding in the bushes. The girls screamed and fought back, but they were dragged from the canoe and taken away on the long journey to the Shawnee villages.

There was great excitement in Boonesborough when the girls were missed. Two parties set out at once in pursuit. Daniel had raced from his cabin without even stopping to put on his moccasins. There were three young men in the party who were especially anxious, too, for they were in love with the girls.

Pioneer daughters that they were, the girls had done everything they could to make the trail easy to find. They had dug their feet into the ground, they had broken twigs wherever they could, and they had even torn bits of their clothing to drop along the way.

The trail was soon picked up. Then it must have seemed to the other men that Daniel knew every thought the Indians were thinking. He seemed to know every move they would make, every stream they would cross, every place they might stop.

When at last, after a chase of thirty-five miles, the Boonesborough men crept silently up to the Indian camp and saw that the girls were still alive, they were happy indeed! Daniel planned each move carefully so the Indians would not have time to kill their prisoners. His men aimed their guns, and at Boone's signal they fired. Two Indians were killed at once, and the other three escaped into the canebrake.

It was a thrilling rescue, and an adventure with a happy ending. For Betsy Calloway soon married one of her rescuers in the first Kentucky wedding, and the next year, Jemima and Fanny did the same.

Then Daniel himself was captured by the Indians.

Boonesborough needed salt. It is hard for us, who need only to reach for a salt-shaker, to know what salt meant to the settlers. They needed salt to keep their meat—their food supply—from spoiling, and they treasured salt for the extra little taste it gave to the same dull food they ate day after day. It was said that a frontiersman was likely to complain more loudly about being without salt than about being surrounded by Indians!

The settlers made their own salt from the salt springs that were common in Kentucky. These streams and pools of water, rich in salt, were called "licks" because the deer and buffalo came to them to lick greedily for the salt that they, too, needed. Around the "licks" lay the huge white bones of giant animals that had once walked the earth and had once come to lick for their salt at these very springs.

Boonesborough needed salt, so in the cold January of 1778, Daniel and a group of men went out with the big salt kettles to camp at the Blue Licks. Here they worked hard at making their salt, by boiling down the water from the springs.

They were almost ready to return to the settlement. But the salt party still needed food, so Daniel went out to look at his beaver traps. It was a freezing day, and soon it began to snow heavily. Daniel was caught in the snowstorm and captured by the Shawnees.

The Indians were delighted with their prisoner, for Boone was a prize catch. When they took him back to their camp, Daniel was horrified to find that hundreds of warriors in war paint, led by the British, were gathered for an attack on the settlements. He pretended once more to be happy to be with his red-skinned brothers, but there was only one thought in his mind from then on—how to save Boonesborough!

He gained some time for Boonesborough by agreeing to go back to the Blue Licks with the Indians. And he told them that if they promised not to harm his men, he would ask them to surrender. Then, knowing the ways of the Indians, he was able to convince them, now they had so many prisoners, that it would be easier to capture Boonesborough in the spring.

The prisoners were taken to Ohio, to the Indian village of Chillicothe. Boone was a great favorite and he was soon "adopted" into the tribe as the son of the Shawnee chief, Blackfish. Daniel had to pretend he enjoyed the business of being "adopted" but it couldn't have been much fun! Most of his hair was plucked out, he was washed and rubbed in the river to "take all his white blood out," and his body was painted with Shawnee signs. Chief Blackfish then honored Daniel by naming him Sheltowee, Big Turtle, and taking him into his family.

But all this time "Big Turtle" was planning his escape. About four months later, when Daniel saw warriors gathering from many tribes, he knew the war parties would soon be heading for Boonesborough. There was no more time to be lost. Seizing a moment when he was not closely watched, Daniel escaped into the woods and sped for Boonesborough, one hundred sixty miles away. In four days he reached the settlement, where he had already been given up for dead.

He did not return a moment too soon! Boonesborough was in no condition to defend itself. Walls and blockhouses and gates had to be repaired; new walls and two new blockhouses had to be built. The men of Boonesborough got to work at once, strengthening their fort for the expected attack.

The attack did not come immediately. When it did, the settlers found themselves terribly outnumbered. There were well over four hundred Indians, while in the fort there were only some thirty men, about twenty boys, and a number of women and children.

In a battle that lasted ten days, the Indians, advised and aided by the British, used every trick and every weapon to capture or destroy the fort. They kept up a steady gunfire. They tried to climb over the walls of the fort, only to be driven back each time. They threw flaming arrows into the cabins, and if the rains had not come down at night they would have surely burned out the settlers. They dug a tunnel from the river to the fort, planning to blow it up. Luckily, the wet earth caved in and the tunnel could not be used. By the tenth day, ten terrifying days and nights, the people of Boonesborough hardly dared hope they would survive this attack.

Survive they did.

On the eleventh day the Indians gave up.

Boonesborough was saved.

ELBOW ROOM

There were four more years of fearful warfare with the Indians before peace came at last to the Wilderness. Then, with peace, came people— a steady movement of people over the Wilderness Road, coming to make their homes in the land that was no longer a wilderness.

Daniel Boone was a famous man now, known even across the sea as America's great hunter and woodsman. But as he watched Kentucky changing, these were not happy years for Daniel.

He saw the lonely frontier giving way to crowded settlements. He saw cabins going up all around him. He saw people pushing back the great forests he loved, driving away their deer and buffalo. And it soon turned out that there were not only too many people for Daniel, but too many lawyers as well!

He had thought that when he opened the Wilderness, cleared the land, and then through years of peril helped to hold it fast, surely he would have the right to call some of this land his own. But Daniel, who was at home in the deepest forest, found it hard to learn the ways of the town. He had never bothered about the pieces of paper a man

needed to prove in a court of law that land he claimed was really his. Soon he found that those who *did* have the proper pieces of paper had taken all his land away. He was poor again, and in debt to many people.

Once more the "mover" began to feel restless.

There were tales of rich and still uncrowded land to the west, in Missouri, owned then by the Spanish. Some of the old feeling of excitement must have stirred in Daniel again as he listened to those tales. Especially as he was no longer happy among the people in Kentucky

who seemed to have forgotten how much he had done for them.

So Daniel Boone, now sixty-five, set off once more to make a new home on a new frontier. With him went his family and the many friends who were always willing to "go along with Dan'l."

He left Kentucky as a hero, with people coming from afar to see him off. And when someone asked him why he was leaving, he made his famous reply: "Too many people! Too crowded! Too crowded! I want more elbow room!"

In Missouri, welcomed and honored by the Spanish government, Daniel found himself once more in forest lands where the hunting was good. There, too, he visited the Shawnees' camp, and found among his former foes some Indians who remembered him as "Big Turtle." It was a visit made in friendship; for in the woodland life they both loved, there seemed always to be a bond between Daniel Boone and the Indians.

Daniel lived to be a very old man, but his spirit was as young and vigorous as ever. It was just like Daniel Boone to try at the age of seventy-eight to enlist in the War of 1812. He was probably quite angry because he wasn't taken!

In 1817, when he was eighty-three years old, he made a trip back to Kentucky to pay off his debts. He is said to have left then with a feeling of satisfaction—and fifty cents in his pocket.

To the end of his life Daniel remained the skilled hunter and woodsman. As a very old man, he took great pride in showing James Audu-

bon, who became the famous "bird man," that he could still "bark" a squirrel. This was a real marksman's trick. Instead of aiming at the squirrel, you had to aim at the tree right below it, and kill the squirrel by stunning it with a piece of bark!

Daniel explored and hunted and trapped almost until the last years of his life. He wandered through Missouri as he had once wandered through Kentucky, roaming far and wide. It is thought that he may even have reached Yellowstone and the Rockies. At eighty-four, he was still planning to go farther west!

Then, on September 26, 1820, he died, at the age of eighty-six.

The boy who wanted a rifle when he was ten years old had, in his manhood, used it well not only for himself, but also for those countless others of his countrymen for whom he had opened up the Wilderness.

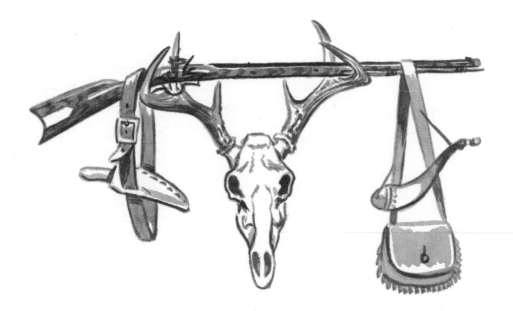

Other titles in this series

Published by

RANDOM HOUSE, 457 Madison Avenue, New York 22, N. Y.